A closer look at me
and our place wi...

WHO'S I...

FRIEND
ZONE

By JonKeL

Who's In Your Friend Zone

JonKeL

Published by JonKeL, 2024.

While every precaution has been taken in the preparation of this book, the publisher assumes no responsibility for errors or omissions, or for damages resulting from the use of the information contained herein.

WHO'S IN YOUR FRIEND ZONE

First edition. November 8, 2024.

Copyright © 2024 JonKeL.

ISBN: 979-8227978585

Written by JonKeL.

Also by JonKeL

Trauma Monsters: A Collection of Poetry
Trauma Monsters: The Breakdowns
Who's In Your Friend Zone
Joints With 2 J's

To the friends who call themselves family, the ones who've shown what trust, loyalty, and love truly mean. To those who've stood by someone through their toughest times and celebrated their highest moments, thank you for being the unwavering support that only a FRIEND can be.

See the problem most face with friendships is fear.

Afraid to let anyone in,

But building up walls can leave you feeling trapped too.

Brick by brick, I've learned to build

a home within my homies.

A place to vent when the pressure becomes too much.

A shoulder to lean on when a crutch ain't enough.

Sometimes it takes many seasons to cultivate a kinship.

And some friendships can be fertilized with faith.

And That's how you make your miracle grow.

All I know is this,

The thought of me being me without my besties,

Just doesn't exist.

Introduction

This book touches on the evolving understanding of friendship and its profound impact on mental health and overall well-being. From a young age, I was introduced to the concept of "friendship" without fully grasping what it meant. Often, friendships are about play and convenience early on. But as we grow, we realize true friendships require deeper qualities: trust, empathy, and mutual support.

The decision to examine my friendships reflects a meaningful approach to self-discovery. Friendships can mirror our values, self-worth, and boundaries. In exploring "Who's In Your Friend Zone," you're actually peeling back layers of your own identity, worth, and aspirations.

Science supports the idea that strong, supportive relationships are crucial for mental health and longevity. Research shows that those with reliable friends or community connections tend to have lower stress, better resilience, and a reduced risk of mental health challenges. Friends provide a safety net, offering emotional support that allows us to process difficult times, celebrate achievements, and experience a sense of togetherness.

My personal experience coming from a toxic family environment highlights how friendships can fill emotional gaps and create positive growth. Many who come from challenging family backgrounds as I did, find solace and healing in friendships. I'm glad I had the opportunity to tell my friends that without them, I wouldn't be the man I am today. These relationships teach us that trust, care, and respect are possible—and they show us a healthier version of "family."

While building meaningful friendships can be challenging, it's clear they're worth the effort. Friends add richness and support, contribute to our well-being, and even extend our life expectancy. So, nurturing these bonds is more than a social activity; it's a form of self-care that helps us live better, fuller lives.

Best Friends

Being someone's best friend is a serious commitment that goes beyond companionship. It's not about titles. "Besties" isn't a badge to be displayed on social media posts for likes and views. It's a partnership of trust, loyalty, and understanding, where each person offers genuine support and care for the other's well-being. This kind of friendship allows each person to fully be themselves, confident in knowing that they'll be accepted—even embraced—for their flaws and vulnerabilities. When life brings joy, a best friend celebrates with you; when it brings hardship, they stand by your side, offering comfort and stability.

However, true friendship is a mutual responsibility. Everything you want in a best friend—patience, empathy, trustworthiness, and loyalty—are qualities you must also embody. It's a two-way street, where each person meets the other halfway, creating a balanced and lasting bond.

But a friendship of this caliber doesn't develop overnight. In the age of instant gratification, most don't have the patience to embark on the journey of a relationship of this nature. The pursuit of this happiness can seem elusive. Building a best friendship is much like constructing a sturdy wall. It takes time, intention, and care, with each interaction forming a new brick. Rushed connections often crumble, lacking the foundation needed to weather life's inevitable storms. Yet, those built with patience and sincerity become unshakeable.

Reflecting on my own journey with friendships, I've been fortunate to share this kind of connection with only a select few. My first best friend came into my life during my early adolescence, and our friendship spanned about a decade before life took us in different directions. The second began at 15, and over 25 years later, we're still close—a friendship that has matured and deepened over time. My most recent best friend came into my life only eight years ago, and our bond continues to grow stronger every day. I feel truly blessed to have had each of these friends, as they've shaped and enriched my life in ways that words can't fully capture.

Can money impact the friendship?

Best friends often share everything, from clothes to memories, and sometimes, financial help. But when it comes to lending or borrowing money, even the strongest friendships require caution. Money can be a complicated and sensitive issue, even in relationships grounded in trust. While it may seem natural to want to help a friend financially, especially when they're in need, it's important to set boundaries that protect both your friendship and your finances.

Money issues can easily create tension, misunderstandings, or even resentment. If a friend struggles to pay you back, the emotional impact can be as damaging as the financial loss. Growing up, I witnessed my own mom lose friends because of money. It's painful to feel like you've lost a friend over money, or that a financial transaction has overshadowed your bond. Therefore, before lending, it's wise to consider a few questions: Can you afford to lend this amount? Are you comfortable with the possibility it may not be repaid? How will this affect your friendship if repayment is delayed or forgotten?

I've loaned and borrowed money from close friends, but I understand that not everyone has the same financial resources. For some people, lending even a small amount might be a big ask, while others may have the means to loan larger sums without much thought. To me, there's really no such thing as "small money"—every dollar has value, especially when trust and friendship are involved. But the amount does matter in terms of how we approach these kinds of exchanges and the trust that comes with them.

When I was 19, I experienced firsthand the power of someone else's generosity. A coworker—someone I wouldn't even consider a close friend—loaned me $1,000 for a down payment on a car. I was floored by their willingness to help, especially at that scale, and I felt a deep sense of responsibility to honor that trust. We set clear terms, and I was careful to repay the loan over several months, bit by bit. That experience taught me a lot about the nuances of lending and borrowing, especially among friends and coworkers, and how crucial it is to follow through on commitments.

In my view, a small loan is anything under $250—an amount I could part with fairly easily if a friend was in need. A loan of $500 falls into a middle tier where I'd need to weigh the situation carefully, considering not only the friend's circumstances but also my own. When it comes to $1,000 or more, though, that's a serious commitment. I'd only lend that to a "ride-or-die" friend, someone I have a deep bond with and trust completely.

Setting clear terms up front can go a long way when it comes to lending—or giving—money to friends. Even a casual discussion about repayment plans can help prevent misunderstandings down the road. It doesn't have to be a formal contract, but having a mutual understanding of when and how the money will be repaid shows respect for both parties. If you intend it as a gift rather than a loan, make that clear from the beginning, so there's no lingering expectation of repayment on your end or confusion on theirs.

This level of open, honest communication might feel awkward at first, but it can prevent small issues from becoming fractures in the friendship. Setting boundaries around money, especially with those we care about, is crucial for preserving the relationship. It's about making sure everyone's on the same page, so there are no unexpected surprises or resentments building up over time.

When people avoid these conversations, they can end up in a cycle of frustration and hurt feelings, with the original generosity turning bittersweet. And, as we've all seen, even the best intentions can spiral into dramatic outcomes. If things go wrong, you don't want to find yourself arguing over fifty bucks in front of a judge on one of those court TV shows. A little honesty now can help keep the friendship healthy, respectful, and out of the courtroom.

In the end, while financial support may sometimes be a loving gesture, it's worth remembering that friendship is ultimately about connection, not obligation. By treating financial boundaries with respect, you protect the bond you share from one of the most common sources of stress. A true friend will appreciate and understand this care for both your relationship and your individual well-being.

Lesson 1: Gratitude

Gratitude, though often perceived as a simple acknowledgment, can significantly transform friendships. It encourages us to notice and appreciate small gestures, shared experiences, and support, which often pass by unremarked. By expressing gratitude, we elevate these ordinary moments, reinforcing the unique bond we share with our friends. This practice not only deepens loyalty and fulfillment but also builds a foundation of mutual respect, which helps friendships endure through challenges.

In my experience, gratitude played a powerful role in my upbringing. During my teenage years, when I faced homelessness, gratitude was a key part of my resilience and survival. This ability to appreciate kindness, help, or even just moments of solace became an abundant source of strength. It also helped me discover a sense of compassion, enabling me to see the humanity in others and to hold onto the spirit of connection despite difficult circumstances.

Here are a few ways to bring gratitude into your friendships:

1. Express Specific Thanks

- Take a moment to acknowledge specific things your friend has done, however small. This specificity shows you're paying attention and truly appreciate them.

2. Share Memories

- Taking a trip down memory lane can be a fun ride indeed. Reminiscing over shared moments with a positive spin can remind both of you of the good times you've had together, enhancing the bond.

3. Be Present

- Show gratitude through attentiveness. Listen actively, celebrate their achievements, and be there for them during tough times.

4. Write a Note

- In a digital world, a handwritten note expressing what they mean to you can be very meaningful.

Gratitude becomes a practice that strengthens friendships and brings compassion and understanding into each interaction.

Activity: Write a letter to a close friend expressing gratitude, which you can later share or keep for yourself.

Colleagues and Coworkers

After three decades in the workforce, I've had the opportunity to work alongside a broad spectrum of colleagues, each bringing unique experiences, personalities, and work styles to the table. I've shared moments of blood, sweat, and tears with coworkers across various high-stakes settings, from drawing blood as a phlebotomist in healthcare to reaching out to underserved communities in nonprofits, and serving in the military until an injury ended my time in service.

In healthcare, I learned firsthand that teamwork can make or break your day. There, we often worked in challenging conditions, facing situations where quick thinking and mutual support were necessary. My time as a phlebotomist taught me to stay calm under pressure, especially when patients were anxious or fearful. Coworkers were often the ones helping us through those long shifts, offering a quick joke to break the monotony or an extra hand in those moments when every minute felt like a marathon.

In the nonprofit sector, I saw another side of collaborative work. As an outreach worker, we were a small but dedicated team, each of us driven by the mission of helping others, often in situations where resources were stretched thin. Here, support from colleagues wasn't just a nice-to-have—it was essential. Whether we were brainstorming ways to reach more people, sharing ideas, or covering for each other on the front lines, our connection helped keep us going through some truly demanding days.

And then there was the military, where the environment was highly structured yet carried its own intense challenges. After sustaining an injury that led to my departure, I came to understand how much these bonds with colleagues truly mattered. The pressure in that environment required a different level of trust and dependability, where knowing your teammates had your back could mean the difference between success and failure—or even safety and danger.

Although those were just a few jobs I held, across all of these roles, I've come to realize that the support of colleagues is invaluable. No matter the setting, when people work together with mutual respect and a shared goal, they can push through almost any challenge. The relationships I built in each of these fields didn't just help me succeed—they taught me the true meaning of collaboration.

Being a coworker goes beyond working side-by-side; it requires communication, shared responsibilities, and a commitment to achieving the team's goals. Even though workplace relationships may not always develop into deep personal connections, they still require mutual respect and cooperation. This professional respect creates a supportive atmosphere where people feel valued, motivated, and able to contribute to collective success. Over time, this sense of camaraderie often leads to what we might call "work friends."

But when you're working full-time, the boundary between professional and personal can blur. Spending a large portion of your day with coworkers, celebrating milestones like birthdays and anniversaries, offering condolences during hard times, and bonding over post-work happy hours can make it feel like these relationships extend beyond work. In these moments, it's natural to ask whether these people are truly friends or simply "friends at work"—a relationship often defined by the shared experience of your work environment rather than a lasting personal bond.

Having to assess this line can be challenging, especially if a job change, project shift, or personal situation arises.

Sometimes, those we call "friends" at work remain just that—friends within the bounds of the workplace, with feelings that are only tied to shared projects, daily routines, and mutual responsibilities. Once that shared environment is gone, we may lose touch, not out of animosity but simply because our lives and paths diverge. However, every so often, a work connection goes beyond just collaboration and becomes a lasting friendship, one that withstands time, distance, and even changes in life circumstances.

One such friendship for me is with my former boss, Andi, from the clinic, where we worked side by side for ten years. In those years, we became more than just colleagues—we became partners in a shared mission to make a positive impact on our community. The clinic's work was demanding, with endless hours of testing, counseling, and educating people from all over the tri-county area about Hepatitis C and other infectious diseases.

By age 25, I worked my way up to a supervisor position, as project coordinator, which wasn't an easy feat. Andi trusted me to take on more responsibilities, and together we developed programs, organized outreach events, and faced the everyday challenges of running a clinic. Through the stress of the work, we leaned on each other, pushing through long days because we knew that what we were doing mattered.

Our friendship grew through those years, built on respect and the deep understanding that comes from seeing each other's strengths and struggles firsthand. Even after moving on from the clinic, that connection stayed strong because, in a way, we built something lasting together.

She was there through a significant chapter of my life, even attending my wedding. More than a decade after the company folded, we're still in touch, proving that some workplace bonds go well beyond the walls of the office. This relationship wasn't always easy or straightforward.

In the beginning, our dynamic was understandably complex, with lines blurred between "boss" and "friend." Navigating that balance took effort and clear communication, especially during tough times when the professional hierarchy came into play. There were moments when she had to make difficult calls as a supervisor, and I had to respect those decisions, even if they affected me personally.

Working through those complexities strengthened our bond. We learned to respect each other's roles, to support one another professionally while maintaining a genuine friendship. That effort to navigate boundaries ultimately created a foundation of trust, mutual respect, and shared history that helped our friendship endure. Now, looking back, I'm grateful we took the time to work through those blurred lines. It taught me that workplace friendships, while sometimes complicated, can evolve into some of the most meaningful connections in life.

In either case, what matters is the authenticity of the bond during the time you shared, whether it remains within the workplace or grows outside of the cubicle into a deeper friendship. This self-reflection can also remind you of the unique and lasting impact coworkers have on your life, even if only during that brief chapter.

Lesson 2: Friendship Inventory

The concept of "quality over quantity" in friendships highlights the value of a few close, meaningful connections over a large circle of acquaintances. While it can be tempting to build an extensive social network, driven by the idea that more friends might offer more opportunities or support, real friendship isn't about numbers. True connections aren't measured by the size of your group but by the depth of your bonds. It's about those few people who genuinely understand you, who stand by you through thick and thin, and who you trust without reservation.

For me, I've never felt the need to surround myself with an entourage. Whether it's my social media following or the number of contacts in my phone, I don't measure my social life by quantity. I've always been more comfortable with a small circle of close friends, those few people I know I can rely on and who genuinely care about me. Large gatherings or endless socializing often leave me feeling drained, but a deep conversation with a close friend can definitely give me life.

These close friendships feel like a safe haven. When I'm with my core group, there's no need to put on a facade or keep up appearances. We can share our struggles, hopes, and even our flaws, knowing that judgment has no place in these relationships. It's a mutual trust that allows us to be open and vulnerable, which is something I wouldn't trade for any number of superficial connections.

In a world where people often equate popularity with success or validation, I'm grateful for my handful of real friends. They're the ones who offer genuine support, who show up when it matters, and who know me well enough to see beyond the surface. To me, these friendships—few as they may be—are worth more than any number of acquaintances could ever offer. In choosing quality over quantity, I've found a sense of belonging that feels both real and complete.

Activity: To determine the quality of your friendships make a list of your closest friends and rate each relationship on a scale of one to ten.

Acquaintances

An acquaintance is someone we recognize and may engage with in certain settings, but the relationship lacks the depth, trust, and closeness we reserve for friends. Interactions with acquaintances are often situational—confined to specific places or events like work, community activities, or occasional gatherings. While these exchanges may be polite and friendly, they generally don't extend beyond surface-level conversations. With acquaintances, there's an unspoken understanding that the connection is casual and isn't expected to progress into deeper emotional territory.

However, it's not uncommon for some acquaintances to blur these boundaries, presenting themselves as friends without truly having built a foundation for that claim. This can be particularly tricky, as it may create the impression of closeness where there is none. I've experienced this firsthand. At a professional training session, I had casual exchanges with a person from a different agency, sharing lunch and perhaps a few polite conversations. But beyond those brief interactions, the relationship never moved past small talk.

You wouldn't believe, in a surprising plot twist, this acquaintance posted a photo from the training on social media with a caption that implied a new friendship. When someone who knew him better warned me about his character, it became clear that this was not a person I wanted to know beyond an acquaintance level. Without getting into the details of the situation, let's just say they could've been on the #metoo list. I wisely chose to remove the tag and ignore the friend request, protecting my boundaries and recognizing that some connections are best left at arm's length.

Navigating relationships with acquaintances requires discernment, especially when your work puts you in the public eye. As a performance artist, I meet a lot of people. Having been on TV, I know how it feels to run into someone who thinks they "know" me, though they only know of me. They've seen a version of me, the one I show to an audience, but that doesn't mean they've seen me.

In the creative world, people often assume you're outgoing or constantly in "performance mode," but many of us are actually introverted. It can surprise people when I mention that. After all, being on stage or in front of a camera requires openness, a willingness to share, but it also takes energy. Whenever I'm out hosting events, performing, or attending book signings, I find myself having to protect that energy. It's a balancing act—creating connections with genuine fans and supporters without giving away too much of myself or feeling too exposed.

I've learned to keep my boundaries firm, knowing that not everyone I meet needs to become a friend or confidant. It's okay to leave some relationships in the casual category and let them stay there. After all, part of maintaining a healthy life is knowing where to draw the line, keeping enough of yourself to recharge, and nurturing those few meaningful connections that genuinely support and understand you.

Some people simply serve a purpose within a specific context, and allowing them to remain at the acquaintance level honors the appropriate distance while still preserving courtesy and professionalism.

Lesson 3: Stay Connected

Staying connected with friends, even in simple ways, is essential for keeping bonds strong and making each other feel valued. Life has a way of pulling us in a million different directions, but friendships need attention to thrive—especially when miles get in the way. When one of my closest friends moved to another state, I realized just how important it was to make a conscious effort to bridge that distance. The little things we do, like sending quick daily texts or tagging each other in funny posts on social media, may seem small, but they're powerful reminders that we're still present in each other's lives.

We also plan trips, whether it's me visiting her or us meeting somewhere halfway. These moments become something to look forward to and remind us that friendship can go beyond geographical maps. The anticipation and the effort we put into making these visits happen reinforce just how much we mean to each other.

Ultimately, you have to prioritize the people you care about. It's easy to let days or even months slip by without reaching out, but a strong friendship is built on intention. Even when life gets busy, taking that extra minute to connect can make all the difference, ensuring that the people who matter most stay a part of your everyday life, no matter where they are in the world.

Here are some practical ways that I use to stay in touch within my friend groups, even if time is tight:

1. Send a Simple Text or Voice Note

- A quick "Hey boo, just thinking of you!" or "What's good with you homie!" text can go a long way. Voice notes can also add a personal touch, letting friends hear your tone and emotion, which can feel more meaningful than typed words alone. My bestie prefers voice notes and since she moved to another state, hearing her voice adds a sense of closeness.

2. Share Memes, Inside Jokes, or News Articles

- Sharing a funny meme, an article that reminds you of an inside joke, or even a random photo is a fun way to keep the connection alive. It doesn't take much time but shows that you're thinking of them and remember what you share in common.

3. Schedule Regular Check-Ins or "Catch-Up" Calls

- For close friends, consider setting a routine, like a monthly catch-up call or coffee date (in person or virtually). It's something both of you can look forward to, and the regularity can help prevent too much time from slipping by without connection.

4. Use Social Media Strategically

- Commenting on their posts, reacting to their stories, or tagging them in something that's "so them" are easy ways to stay connected. Social media offers a way to stay up-to-date with friends' lives, even when you don't have time for a full conversation.

5. Celebrate Milestones and Special Dates

- Remembering birthdays, anniversaries, and other important events is a meaningful way to stay in touch. A short message acknowledging these milestones can make friends feel appreciated and remembered.

6. Plan Small Group Activities, Virtual or In-Person

- Group chats are perfect for quick updates or sharing plans that anyone can join. Planning a virtual game night, happy hour, or in-person brunch gives everyone a chance to reconnect without demanding one-on-one time.

7. Send a Thoughtful Card or Small Gift

- A handwritten note or a small surprise, like their favorite coffee or a book they've wanted to read, can be incredibly heartwarming. Physical gestures like this are rare these days, so they stand out and make friends feel cherished.

8. Keep Track of Their Interests and Reach Out Accordingly

- If a friend is excited about an upcoming event, project, or goal, check in on it later. "How did your presentation go?" or "Did you finish that book?" These questions show that you care about their life and interests.

9. Create or Contribute to a Group Tradition

- Starting a tradition can be a fun, reliable way to stay connected. This could be an annual camping trip, a weekly trivia night, or a monthly group chat session to share updates. Traditions help create shared memories and give everyone something to look forward to.

10. Encourage Open Communication About Busy Times

- Life's demands fluctuate, so being honest about periods when you're busy—and encouraging friends to do the same—helps keep things lighthearted and understanding. Reaching out whenever possible, even with a short message, can keep the friendship going, and friends will feel less pressured if they're also going through a busy time.

Staying connected doesn't always have to be grand or time-consuming. Sometimes it's the little, consistent efforts that mean the most and make friendships feel steady and valued, even when life is busy.

Activity: Make an action plan to reconnect with a friend you value but haven't spoken to recently.

Friends With Benefits

As a millennial with a broad span of life experience across five decades, I've witnessed major cultural shifts in the way relationships are defined and approached. In recent years, there's been a growing openness around "non-committal relationships"—arrangements that satisfy emotional or physical needs without traditional labels or obligations. Among these, "situationships" and platonic intimacy have emerged as notable variations, each serving a unique purpose and meeting different personal needs.

A "situationship," commonly referenced by Gen Z, is a relationship with physical and emotional closeness but without the commitment and label of a traditional relationship. It's a space where people enjoy each other's company and intimacy while still maintaining personal freedom. Meanwhile, "platonic intimacy" explores the importance of deep, affectionate, and often tactile friendships without any sexual element. It emphasizes the value of human touch and closeness—hugging, cuddling, and similar gestures that nurture emotional bonds while preserving boundaries.

Then there's the "friends with benefits" model, which adds a different layer. This arrangement combines friendship with a casual, sexual relationship, clearly agreed upon by both parties to avoid emotional exclusivity. The goal is to share a physical connection without pursuing a deeper, romantic commitment. This setup can be appealing for those who want companionship and intimacy without the demands of a full romantic relationship. However, boundaries are crucial to ensure both parties remain on the same page, as the absence of emotional exclusivity can sometimes create feelings of jealousy or hurt if honesty is compromised.

Other terms—like "no strings attached," "hookup," or "booty call"—are used more commonly to describe purely sexual relationships without a foundation of friendship. In these cases, the focus is on the physical aspect alone, often detached from emotional intimacy or personal connection.

Before I settled down at the ripe age of 20, I had experience with friends-with-benefits relationships, finding it liberating to share companionship, meals, and occasional intimacy without the expectations or demands of a committed relationship. There was an ease in communication, where either person could openly express interest in meeting up, sometimes for intimacy, without strings attached. This arrangement offered a mix of friendship and regular sexual connection in a way that was transparent and mutually understood.

At the core of non-committal relationships, whether they're platonic, sexual, or somewhere in between, is the importance of open communication and mutual understanding. Boundaries need to be maintained, but when handled with honesty, these relationships can meet personal needs in a satisfying way, offering growth and preparation for future committed relationships or even enhancing existing friendships.

Lesson 4: Healthy Boundaries

Setting healthy boundaries with friends is essential for maintaining respectful, balanced, and mutually satisfying relationships. Clear boundaries ensure that both people feel valued and understood, helping to prevent resentment, burnout, and misunderstandings. Here are a few ways to establish and set healthy boundaries with friends:

1. Be Honest About Your Needs

- Openly communicate your needs with friends, whether it's for personal space, time alone, or emotional limits. For example, saying, "I need some time to recharge after work, so I'm not always available to hang out on weekdays," lets friends know your preferences clearly. Honest communication from the start sets the tone for a respectful dynamic.

2. Set Limits on Time and Availability

- Balancing personal time with time for friends can be challenging, but it's important. If you're not available every time they ask to hang out, don't feel pressured to overextend yourself. Politely explain that you value your time and may not always be free but are still interested in staying connected. Learning to say "no" kindly helps maintain a sense of control over your time. This is still a struggle for me but I also know how stressful overextending myself can be.

3. Define Emotional Boundaries

- Recognize and communicate what types of conversations or support are comfortable for you. If a friend leans heavily on you for emotional support, clarify your boundaries. You might say, "I'm here for you, but I may not always have the mental energy to talk about heavy topics. Let's set up a time when I can give you my full attention." This approach shows compassion while protecting your emotional well-being.

4. Be Clear About Financial Boundaries

- As discussed earlier, money can create tension in friendships, so it's helpful to be upfront about finances. For example, if a friend often suggests expensive outings, you could say, "I'd love to spend time together, but I'm keeping an eye on my budget. Let's find some more affordable ways to hang out." This reinforces that you value their friendship without compromising your financial boundaries.

5. Practice Communicating Boundaries Early On

- Bringing up boundaries at the beginning of a friendship can set a respectful foundation. Sharing boundaries as naturally as you would personal interests or goals helps normalize them, so they don't feel like a "big deal" later. For example, saying something like, "I'm a big believer in setting aside personal time for self-care, so I sometimes go offline on weekends" can help friends understand how you operate.

6. Establish Boundaries on Digital Communication

- In today's digital age, it's important to set boundaries on messaging and social media. If constant messages are overwhelming, let friends know that you may not respond immediately, or prefer certain hours for communication. You could say, "I'm trying to limit screen time, so I may not reply right away, but I'll get back to you as soon as I can."

7. Respect Each Other's Boundaries, Too

- Boundaries are a two-way street, so encourage friends to set and share theirs as well. Checking in with, "Is this okay with you?" or "Let me know if you need anything different" can foster a supportive space where both people feel comfortable and respected. Respecting their boundaries reinforces mutual trust and encourages them to respect yours as well.

8. Be Consistent and Hold Firm When Needed

- Once you've set a boundary, it's important to maintain it. If friends test your limits, gently remind them of what you've communicated. Consistency shows that you value both the boundary and the friendship and helps prevent misunderstandings or hurt feelings down the line.

9. Check In and Adjust Boundaries Over Time

- Friendships evolve and grow, and so can boundaries. Periodically check in with friends to see if any adjustments are needed. This doesn't mean constantly revisiting boundaries but being open to discussing changes as they arise.

Healthy boundaries aren't about pushing people away but creating a friendship that's respectful, balanced, and rewarding. Boundaries help preserve the emotional health of both people and ensure that the friendship remains a source of positive support.

Activity: Identify a list of non-negotiables (things that are not open for debate) to help you set healthy boundaries.

Homies and Bros

The terms homies and bros capture two distinct, though sometimes overlapping, types of male friendships. Each term reflects unique aspects of companionship, culture, and identity, revealing subtle yet meaningful differences in how men relate to and interact with their peers.

Homies

The term "homie," originating from "home girl/boy," has roots in hip hop and urban culture. Being someone's homie is a declaration of close friendship, often reflecting a bond rooted in shared experiences, values, or backgrounds. Homies typically share a level of trust and mutual respect that goes beyond casual friendship. This term implies a strong sense of loyalty and support, often likening the relationship to family—a connection that feels dependable and meaningful. Homies are often seen as confidants who stand by each other through ups and downs, reflecting a deep connection that values genuine friendship over surface-level interactions.

For a lot of men, terms like "homie" or "bro" feel more natural than "best friend." It's not just about word choice—it's about sidestepping societal expectations around masculinity, where words like "best friend" can sometimes feel too formal or vulnerable. Calling someone your "homie" respects the depth of the bond without putting a spotlight on it. It's unspoken but understood, honoring the loyalty and emotional connection without a label that feels too intimate.

To me, my homie Rolando isn't just a friend—he's family. We go back almost 30 years, and he's one of the few people on this earth who knows the real me. He stood by my side as my best man at my wedding two decades ago, and he's still here today, just as solid as ever. We've seen each other at our lowest points, moments we don't talk about but don't have to; we just know. There's a rare kind of trust in a friendship like that, one that doesn't require explanations.

Sometimes I think of him as my best friend, though I wouldn't say it to his face—it's just how we work. But "homie" says it all for us, carrying the weight of a bond that's stood the test of time. It's a friendship that doesn't need flowery words to prove its worth; we've been ride-or-die through it all, no labels required.

Bros

On the other hand, "bros" reflect a different dimension of male friendship, one often tied to bro culture. Bro culture, popular in settings like college fraternities, sports teams, or certain workplaces, describes a social environment centered on shared, often hyper-masculine activities and values. It's associated with group bonding over interests like sports, partying, competitiveness, and loyalty to the group. In this context, "bros" are friends who bond over these shared experiences, often in a playful, sometimes exaggerated display of masculinity. Bro culture fosters unity and belonging through activities that reinforce this sense of "brotherhood," like attending sports events, social gatherings, or working and playing hard together.

"Bro culture" often fosters a sense of camaraderie and belonging among those who fit its mold, providing a feeling of unity and support, particularly in intense or challenging environments. However, it also tends to promote a narrow vision of what is acceptable or "cool," which can exclude those who don't share or align with its values. This culture often celebrates a particular brand of toughness, risk-taking, and conformity that can foster strong friendships among its members but may inadvertently (or even intentionally) dismiss inclusivity. When taken to extremes, it can reinforce stereotypes, encourage unhealthy behavior, and contribute to an environment that lacks accountability.

During my brief time in the army, I became immersed in bro culture. It wasn't something I consciously sought out, but in that environment, it was difficult to avoid. As a new member of the group fresh out of high school, I felt pressure to fit in, and following the group mentality seemed like the easiest path. I found myself adopting behaviors that, at the time, felt almost like rites of passage—drinking heavily, smoking, and even falling into patterns of disrespect toward women. These actions were encouraged, implicitly if not explicitly, as markers of fitting in and being "one of the guys." The culture around me made it seem not only normal but almost necessary to act this way to belong.

Looking back, I can see how damaging this environment was, both to myself and to others. It reinforced a narrow, harmful version of masculinity, one that prized toughness over compassion, bravado over self-awareness. It's painful to think about the behaviors I picked up during that time, and even though I'm not proud of that period in my life, it taught me valuable lessons. I realized that this version of "brotherhood" was hollow, built on conformity rather than genuine connection or respect.

In an ironic way, my injury became a form of liberation. While it was painful and brought its own challenges, it also gave me a way out of a toxic environment that I might have otherwise stayed in, continuing down a path I now regret. The injury allowed me to step back, to see that bro culture, while tempting in its promise of family, had taken me further from my values. It gave me the space to rediscover a version of myself that wasn't dependent on meeting these narrow, often harmful expectations. Today, I'm grateful for that exit. It forced me to confront who I really wanted to be and helped me understand the importance of surrounding myself with people who value authenticity and mutual respect over mindless conformity.

At its best, being a bro is about support and friendship, and it can encourage an enjoyable group dynamic. But it's less about deep, individual connection and more about group identity and bonding through shared activities or interests.

In essence, homies are more like a chosen family, with bonds forged through loyalty, trust, and shared values. Bros, on the other hand, represent a social connection that revolves around group identity and shared experiences, with the strength of the relationship relying more on collective rather than individual closeness. Both have their place in male friendships, but each offers a different approach to connection and belonging.

Lesson 5: Core Values

Core values are essential in building meaningful friendships because they represent the deepest aspects of who we are—our beliefs, our sense of right and wrong, and the principles that guide our actions. Friendships built on shared or mutually respected values are often stronger and more resilient because there's a fundamental understanding at the core. When friends align on values, it sets the foundation for trust, empathy, and a genuine appreciation for one another.

For me, my core values are deeply rooted in an old-school Southern upbringing. Much of what I hold dear stems from religious beliefs and generational wisdom passed down in my family. Growing up, I was surrounded by certain ideas about respect, responsibility, and kindness toward others. While I absorbed these values, I also found myself to be more open-minded than some family members. My family, too, was more open-minded than many others in our community, balancing tradition with a willingness to see beyond strict norms.

A powerful example of these values in action was when a close high school friend of mine, began to question his sexuality, came out to his mother, and she responded by kicking him out. My mother, without hesitation, took him in and treated him like her own, giving him the stability and care he needed during such a vulnerable time in his life. She didn't judge or ask questions; she simply acted out of compassion and kindness, values she had instilled in me all my life. This experience brought my friend and I closer than ever. Seeing my family act with such acceptance reinforced the kind of person I wanted to be and the type of relationships I wanted to build. To this day, that friend and I are still in contact, and I credit our bond to the shared experience of seeing true kindness and support in action thanks to my mom.

This experience reminded me that friendship isn't just about having fun or enjoying each other's company; it's about being there in moments of need, respecting each other's struggles, and showing compassion when it's hardest. Finding friends who understand or share these values has been essential in my life, creating bonds that aren't easily broken.

Here's how core values influence the process of selecting friends:

1. Establishing Common Ground

- Core values give us a sense of connection with others who see the world similarly. When we meet people who prioritize similar values—whether it's integrity, kindness, ambition, or open-mindedness—it feels natural to build a friendship. This common ground encourages conversation and shared interests, making it easier to relate to one another.

2. Building Trust and Respect

- Friendships thrive on trust and respect, and shared values reinforce these qualities. For example, if honesty is a core value, choosing friends who also value honesty helps create a safe space where both of you feel free to be yourselves. With mutual respect for each other's principles, the friendship feels authentic and solid.

3. Navigating Conflicts Smoothly

- Conflicts are inevitable in friendships, but shared values help friends work through disagreements with empathy and understanding. If both friends value open communication and empathy, for example, they're likely to resolve issues constructively rather than allowing misunderstandings to damage the relationship. Core values act as a compass, guiding how both friends approach conflict.

4. Creating a Supportive Environment

- Friendships are often a source of support, so having shared values can mean better understanding and encouragement. For instance, if you value personal growth, friends with similar goals will cheer you on and challenge you in a supportive way. These friends understand and reinforce what you're striving for, creating an environment where you feel empowered to pursue your goals.

5. Encouraging Positive Habits

- When core values align, friends are more likely to support positive habits and respect boundaries. For example, if you value work-life balance, friends with similar priorities will understand when you need time for self-care. This shared understanding allows for healthier boundaries, mutual encouragement, and friendships that enhance rather than drain your energy.

6. Fostering Long-Lasting Connections

- Friendships based on shared values are more likely to endure over time, as values often remain steady even as circumstances change. If two people both value loyalty or compassion, for instance, those qualities can anchor the friendship, helping it weather long distance, life changes, or other challenges.

7. Promoting Self-Reflection and Growth

- Having friends who align with your values encourages you to reflect on your own priorities and stay true to your beliefs. They can help you maintain your values and even inspire personal growth. By seeing them live out shared values, you're motivated to stay committed to what matters to you.

8. Establishing a Meaningful "Inner Circle"

- When selecting friends who resonate with your values, you're intentionally building a meaningful inner circle. This isn't just about surrounding yourself with similar people; it's about creating a network of individuals who uplift, challenge, and support each other in meaningful ways. These are the friends you'll turn to for advice, guidance, and mutual celebration of life's milestones.

Core values act as a filter, guiding us to friends who are aligned with our worldview and aspirations. They help ensure that friendships are not only enjoyable but also enriching, providing mutual support, authenticity, and encouragement to stay true to what matters most.

ACTIVITY: CONSIDER what core values are most important to you, and do your friendships align with them? Make a list and discuss it with your friends.

Ride or Die

The term "ride or die" represents an unparalleled level of loyalty and commitment in relationships, whether between friends, family members, or romantic partners. Originating in hip-hop culture, it signifies someone who is willing to support, stand by, and even sacrifice for another person, regardless of the challenges or dangers that may arise. This is not just an ordinary friendship or partnership; it's a bond that implies enduring trust, dedication, and sometimes even extreme sacrifice.

The phrase "ride or die" suggests a level of devotion that's almost life-or-death—an individual who would metaphorically, and sometimes literally, go to any lengths for the person they care about. It's easy to think of a best friend or significant other as a ride-or-die partner, but the intensity of this commitment is significant. While a best friend might provide emotional support, a "ride or die" would take it a step further, standing by your side no matter the cost, even in life altering situations like taking the blame or accepting consequences on your behalf.

This level of loyalty demands selflessness and resilience. Being someone's ride-or-die requires a willingness to put their well-being above your own, even when it may have real consequences for your own life. It's a role that isn't handed out lightly and isn't something to take on if there's any doubt about your capacity to stand firm, regardless of the cost. Many people use the term casually, but the weight of being a true ride-or-die is intense—it's about loyalty that can withstand legal trouble, danger, or even social backlash, much like taking a charge for someone you trust to take care of your family in return.

For some, this bond might develop with a best friend, a sibling, or a life partner, yet it doesn't automatically apply to everyone in these roles.

A true ride-or-die relationship goes beyond close friendship or love; it requires deep, mutual understanding, trust, and a level of commitment that's rare. It's about knowing that, even in the most extreme circumstances, that person has your back, and you have theirs, fully and unconditionally.

In my opinion, "ride or die" is the highest form of loyalty, where one's dedication to another person transcends typical friendship or companionship. It's an extraordinary commitment, reflecting the kind of relationship where, without hesitation, you'd be willing to face adversity, sacrifice, and even bodily harm for someone else.

Lesson 6: Balanced Communication

Balanced communication (both talking and listening) is essential for nurturing healthy friendships because it builds trust, respect, and understanding. Here's why this balance is so important:

1. Fosters Mutual Understanding

- Good communication goes both ways. Sharing openly and actively listening allows friends to truly understand each other's thoughts, feelings, and experiences. Listening intently, rather than just waiting to speak, helps you pick up on subtle emotions or concerns, which makes the other person feel valued and heard.

2. Builds Trust and Respect

- When friends feel listened to, they're more likely to open up, which strengthens trust. It shows that you're genuinely interested in them, not just in sharing your own thoughts. This creates a safe space where both people can express themselves honestly, knowing they'll be met with respect and empathy.

3. Promotes Empathy and Support

- Listening helps you understand where your friend is coming from and what they need in that moment—whether it's advice, encouragement, or just a compassionate ear. Offering your perspective without dominating the conversation and listening without judging creates a balanced dynamic of support.

4. Strengthens Problem-Solving

- In conflicts or misunderstandings, balanced communication is key to finding solutions. By truly listening to each other, friends can address underlying issues rather than just reacting to surface-level disagreements. This approach keeps small conflicts from becoming big ones and helps friendships withstand challenges.

5. Creates a Fair and Equal Connection

- Friendships thrive when both people feel they have a voice. When one person dominates conversations, the other can feel undervalued or ignored. By both talking and listening, friendships become more balanced and equal, where each person feels respected and engaged in the relationship.

6. Allows for Personal Growth

- Friends help each other grow, and this growth often happens through honest communication. By sharing your thoughts and being open to hearing theirs, you expand each other's perspectives, which is crucial for personal and relational growth.

7. Strengthens Emotional Intimacy

- Open and balanced communication fosters emotional intimacy, as both people feel safe to be vulnerable and honest. The more friends feel they can share and be genuinely heard, the deeper and more meaningful the friendship becomes.

For the most part, communication in friendships is a dance of both talking and listening. This balance keeps both people engaged, appreciated, and understood. By valuing both sides, friends create a deeper, more impactful connection that supports and enriches both lives.

Activity: Write down three ways you can be a better listener with your friends.

Work Spouse

A "work spouse" relationship is a unique dynamic that often arises between colleagues who work closely together and develop a strong, supportive connection. This bond can resemble the understanding, familiarity, and loyalty seen in a marriage, hence the humorous label of "work spouse." This relationship usually involves open communication, shared inside jokes, and mutual support, often offering a dependable source of encouragement through the highs and lows of workplace life.

However, the term "work spouse" can sometimes raise questions in both personal and professional contexts. For the relationship to stay healthy and positive, it's essential to maintain clear boundaries, ensuring it remains strictly platonic and transparent. A work spouse relationship that's balanced and respectful, with no romantic undertones, can be an incredible source of support—someone who knows your daily stresses, can celebrate your wins, and offer a perspective that others outside the workplace might not fully understand, even your real spouse.

This dynamic doesn't necessarily translate outside the work setting. For instance, work spouses may lose touch if one leaves the company or changes roles. The connection is often closely tied to the shared experiences of the job, so it might naturally fade once that bond isn't reinforced by regular interaction. In some cases, though, the connection can evolve into a long-term friendship that extends beyond work, as I've experienced with one of my work spouses who I'm still in touch with after we left the job 13 years ago. However, the other faded when the job ended, highlighting that while meaningful, this type of relationship can also be situational.

Professionally, work spouse relationships may need careful navigating due to HR policies on workplace relationships. Even when a spouse or partner is comfortable with the work spouse connection, colleagues and HR might still monitor it to ensure it aligns with standards of workplace professionalism.

Ultimately, a work spouse can make the workday feel lighter and more manageable. The relationship, when healthy, serves as a supportive, morale-boosting connection that can benefit both parties in their professional lives, as long as everyone involved is clear about the boundaries and intentions.

Lesson 7: Building Trust

Building trust with friends is essential for creating strong, lasting relationships. Trust develops over time through consistent actions, honest communication, and genuine care. Here are some effective tips for building and strengthening trust with friends:

1. Be Reliable and Consistent

- Show up for your friends, especially when you've committed to something. Reliability builds trust because it shows your friend they can count on you. Whether it's meeting plans or following through on a promise, being dependable strengthens the bond.

2. Listen Actively and Empathetically

- Listening is a powerful way to build trust. Give your full attention, avoid interrupting, and show empathy for what your friend is sharing. Active listening makes friends feel heard, valued, and respected, fostering trust.

3. Be Honest, Even When It's Hard

- Honesty forms the foundation of trust. Be open about your feelings, thoughts, and intentions. If you need to give constructive feedback or talk about something sensitive, do so gently and with respect, but always prioritize the truth.

4. Respect Boundaries and Privacy

- Honor your friend's boundaries and keep their private matters confidential. Respecting what they share with you builds trust, as it shows you value their boundaries and will protect their confidences.

5. Show Empathy and Understanding

- Trust grows when friends feel understood and supported. Show empathy by validating their emotions, even if you don't fully understand them. This strengthens your connection and makes your friend feel safe sharing with you.

6. Own Up to Mistakes and Apologize Sincerely

- If you make a mistake, acknowledge it honestly and offer a genuine apology. Taking responsibility for your actions, instead of deflecting blame, shows humility and integrity, which builds trust in the long run.

7. Communicate Openly and Regularly

- Open, honest communication helps prevent misunderstandings and keeps the relationship healthy. Regularly check in with your friend, ask about their life, and share updates from yours. Frequent and meaningful conversations build familiarity and deepen trust.

8. Be Patient and Allow Trust to Grow Gradually

- Trust takes time, so don't rush the process. Give yourself and your friend time to bond and grow closer naturally. Gradual trust-building leads to stronger, more genuine relationships that are resilient over time.

9. Celebrate Their Successes and Support Their Growth

- Show that you're genuinely happy for their achievements and willing to support their growth. A trustworthy friend cheers on your successes without jealousy, adding to a sense of security and loyalty in the friendship.

10. Act with Integrity

- Consistently act in line with your values and principles. Let your friend see that your actions match your words and that you're reliable in all areas. Being a person of integrity instills confidence and reinforces trust in the friendship.

Building trust is a gradual process, but the rewards are invaluable. By prioritizing honesty, empathy, and consistency, you create a strong foundation that will help your friendship thrive.

Activity: Draw a "Trust Tree." Based on level of trustworthiness, place your friends on branches ranging from lowest to the very top to visually see where your strongest bonds are.

Cyber Friend

Back in the day, the concept of a "pen pal" was a popular way to connect with someone across distances, sharing thoughts and details about daily life through handwritten letters. A pen pal relationship requires time, patience, and a level of dedication that feels both nostalgic and somewhat rare in our fast-paced world today. The charm of writing letters, sending postcards, and eagerly awaiting a reply added a sense of anticipation and excitement, as well as an opportunity for personal reflection in a way that few modern communications allow. I had a pen pal in grade school, which was an experience that remains memorable today.

Pen pals have largely evolved into "cyber pals," thanks to advances in technology and the development of social media, messaging apps, and forums. People can now meet and communicate instantly, sharing their lives through text, video, or even voice chat. Online friendships are formed through shared interests in forums, gaming communities, and social networks, allowing people from all walks of life to bond and connect over common interests.

A childhood friend of mine, Brandon, who just celebrated ten years of marriage, met his spouse on an online dating platform. Their relationship began as a cyber connection and grew into a deeply fulfilling and committed partnership, leading to marriage and a beautiful family. This story shows that real, lasting bonds can absolutely form in the digital space.

However, it's essential to stay vigilant in online interactions. Not everyone is who they claim to be, and some may use false identities—a practice known as "catfishing"—to manipulate others, whether for financial gain, emotional control, or simply to create drama. In extreme cases, these deceptions can lead to serious consequences, impacting mental health, trust, and even personal safety.

To navigate online friendships safely, it's wise to protect personal information and set clear boundaries. Avoid sharing details like your home address, financial info, or sensitive personal experiences early in the friendship. Take time to verify the person's identity if the relationship starts to feel significant; video calls or trusted social media connections can help add a layer of authenticity.

Remember that it's okay to question things that don't add up or feel off. Healthy boundaries allow you to enjoy online connections without putting yourself at unnecessary risk. By staying cautious, you can ensure that your cyber friendships remain positive, authentic, and enriching experiences.

Cyber friendships, while often meaningful, may lack some of the depth that can come with in-person connections. Physical presence allows for non-verbal communication, shared activities, and a sense of immediacy that strengthens relationships. Yet, even with these limitations, many people find their online friends to be supportive and uplifting presences in their lives.

Lesson 8: Overcoming Failed Friendships

By now, I hope I've given you some valuable tools to recognize the different types of friendships in your life and strategies for nurturing them in healthier ways. Relationships, even the closest friendships, are rarely without flaws. Perfection isn't the goal; it's about working together to safeguard the qualities we treasure in one another.

When a friendship truly matters, it's worth going the distance, going all twelve rounds—fighting for it, working through challenges, and investing time and care. However, sometimes, despite our best efforts, things just don't work out. Ending a friendship can be incredibly painful, especially when it leaves us feeling like we've lost a part of ourselves. It's natural to grieve this loss, but it's crucial not to let that pain harden us. Becoming jaded only builds walls, walls that can keep out the potential for future connections.

With that in mind, here are a few tips to help you heal from the hurt of a failed friendship and open up to new, meaningful connections

1. Acknowledge Your Feelings

- Take the time to feel and process the disappointment or sadness. Ignoring these emotions often leads to unresolved hurt that can clou future relationships.

2. Reflect on What You've Learned

- Every friendship, good or bad, offers lessons. Think about what you valued and what you might approach differently in the future. Growth often stems from these reflections.

3. Avoid Blaming Yourself or the Other Person

- Friendships, like any relationship, involve two people, each with unique perspectives. Sometimes, things just fall apart naturally, without either party being "at fault."

4. Forgive and Let Go

- Letting go isn't about forgetting; it's about accepting that things unfolded the way they did and forgiving any hurt involved—both theirs and yours.

5. Be Open to New Connections

- When you're ready, put yourself out there again. Building friendships requires vulnerability, and it's okay to approach new connections slowly.

Friendships will come and go, but the lessons we gain and the openness we carry forward will continue to enrich our lives forever.

Activity: Create an action plan to help you make new connections.

Don't miss out!

Visit the website below and you can sign up to receive emails whenever JonKeL publishes a new book. There's no charge and no obligation.

https://books2read.com/r/B-A-HWHX-PRDHF

BOOKS 2 READ

Connecting independent readers to independent writers.

Did you love *Who's In Your Friend Zone*? Then you should read *Trauma Monsters: A Collection of Poetry*[1] by JonKeL!

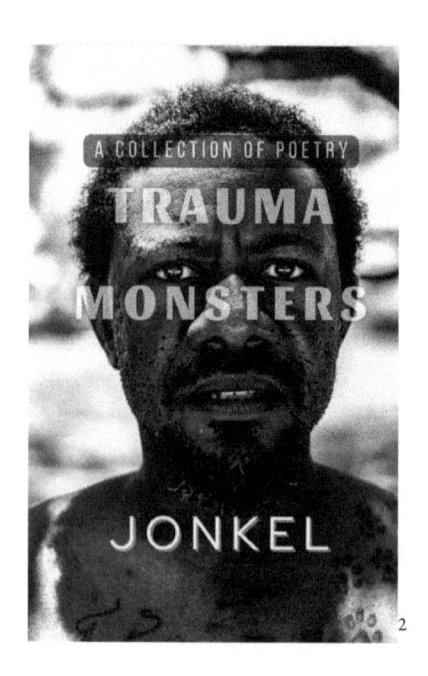

[2]

(Eccentrich @Be.Eccentrich.Inc) "When Jon told me he was writing a book, I knew it would be filled with incredible poems that told amazing stories about a tough childhood deserving of redemption, so I was excited to read it."

(Jacob Mayberry @BlackChakra88) "Everyday I gain more respect for JonKeL. He's someone that's worked for his national ranking. He's someone that consistently works for how good he is in poetry."

(Nick Fury @NickFuryThePoet) "Since JonKeL has been mentoring me, I've grown as an artist significantly. He provided a space for me to share, give me feedback that was more nuanced, and challenged me to

---

1. https://books2read.com/u/4Noz5J

2. https://books2read.com/u/4Noz5J

explore my vulnerabilities through my writing. He always encourages me to find my most authentic voice."

The author invites readers to enter his world through powerful poetry. Trauma Monsters: A Collection of Poetry contains 23 dynamic poems that also includes additional information about each piece. This will provide more insight on the author's creative process and the monsters he's been trying to put to rest. We are often haunted by our past traumas, and sometimes the healthiest coping comes in the form of poetic expression.

Jonathan David Kelly, better known as JonKeL, is a South Florida actor, writer, and creative director. His artistic journey began as a child, winning essay and poetry contests in grade school. Inspired by his father who was also a poet, he connected with this genre of writing for its healing properties, after journaling turned into therapy. It became the healthy, creative outlet he needed to deal with life's struggles. Writing about subjects most youth are too young to process, like domestic violence and drug abuse, creative expression was his first remedy for dealing with the pain.

Also by JonKeL

Trauma Monsters: A Collection of Poetry
Trauma Monsters: The Breakdowns
Who's In Your Friend Zone
Joints With 2 J's